Countries We Come From

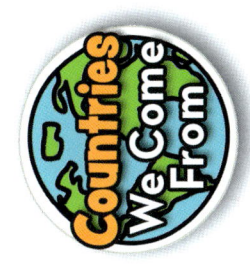

Myanmar

by Anastasiya Vasilyeva

Consultant: Marjorie Faulstich Orellana, PhD
Professor of Urban Schooling
University of California, Los Angeles

BEARPORT PUBLISHING

New York, New York

Credits

Cover, © sirikorn thamniyom/Shutterstock and © franck1508/Shutterstock; 3, © Photomontage/Shutterstock; 4, © Sean Pavone/Alamy; 5T, © Kobby Dagan/Dreamstime; 5B, © M2020/Shutterstock; 7, © eFesenko/Shutterstock; 8, © Sailko3p/Dreamstime; 9T, © Nikada/iStock; 9B, © Varts/Shutterstock; 10T, © Witthaya Khampanant/Alamy; 10B, © Karen de Mamiel/iStock; 11, © chingkai huang/iStock; 12–13, © SeanPavonePhoto/iStock; 13R, © Genius Studio/Shutterstock; 14, © Pictures from History/Bridgeman Images; 15, © ZUMA Press, Inc./Alamy; 16, © Hemis/Alamy; 17T, © SeanPavonePhoto/iStock; 17B, © Volker Preusser/mauritius images/AGE Fotostock; 18, © James Strachan/robertharding/Alamy; 19, © Mlenny/iStock; 20, © SasinTipchai/Shutterstock; 21, © 1001nights/iStock; 22, © Fanfo/Shutterstock; 23, © orientalprincess/Shutterstock; 23T, © Eitan Simanor/robertharding/Alamy; 24, © Xinhua/Sipa USA/Newscom; 25, © Eric Lafforgue/AGE Fotostock; 25T, © Pla2na/Shutterstock; 26, © hadynyah/iStock; 26 Background, © titoOnz/Shutterstock; 27, © Cristina Stoian/Dreamstime; 28–29, © amnat30/Shutterstock; 28B, © Soe Zeya Tun/Reuters/Newscom; 30T, © szefei/Shutterstock and © Fat Jackey/Shutterstock; 30B, © Blanscape/Shutterstock; 31 (T to B), © milosk50/Shutterstock, © Handoko Ramawidjaya Bumi/Shutterstock, © Natanael Alfredo Nemanita Ginting/Dreamstime, © Boriiak/Shutterstock, and © Beer5020/Shutterstock; 32, © Galyamin Sergej/Shutterstock.

Publisher: Kenn Goin
Senior Editor: Joyce Tavolacci
Creative Director: Spencer Brinker
Design: Debrah Kaiser
Photo Researcher: Thomas Persano

Library of Congress Cataloging-in-Publication Data

Names: Vasilyeva, Anastasiya, author.
Title: Myanmar / by Anastasiya Vasilyeva.
Description: New York, New York : Bearport Publishing, 2019. | Series: Countries we come from | Includes bibliographical references and index.
Identifiers: LCCN 2018044160 (print) | LCCN 2018044963 (ebook) | ISBN 9781642802641 (ebook) | ISBN 9781642801958 (library)
Subjects: LCSH: Burma—Juvenile literature.
Classification: LCC DS527.4 (ebook) | LCC DS527.4 .V37 2019 (print) | DDC 959.1—dc23
LC record available at https://lccn.loc.gov/2018044160

Copyright © 2019 Bearport Publishing Company, Inc. All rights reserved. No part of this publication may be reproduced in whole or in part, stored in any retrieval system, or transmitted in any form or by any means, electronic, mechanical, photocopying, recording, or otherwise, without written permission from the publisher.

For more information, write to Bearport Publishing Company, Inc., 45 West 21st Street, Suite 3B, New York, New York 10010. Printed in the United States of America.

10 9 8 7 6 5 4 3 2 1

Contents

This Is Myanmar 4
Fast Facts 30
Glossary 31
Index 32
Read More 32
Learn More Online 32
About the Author 32

Beautiful

This Is Myanmar

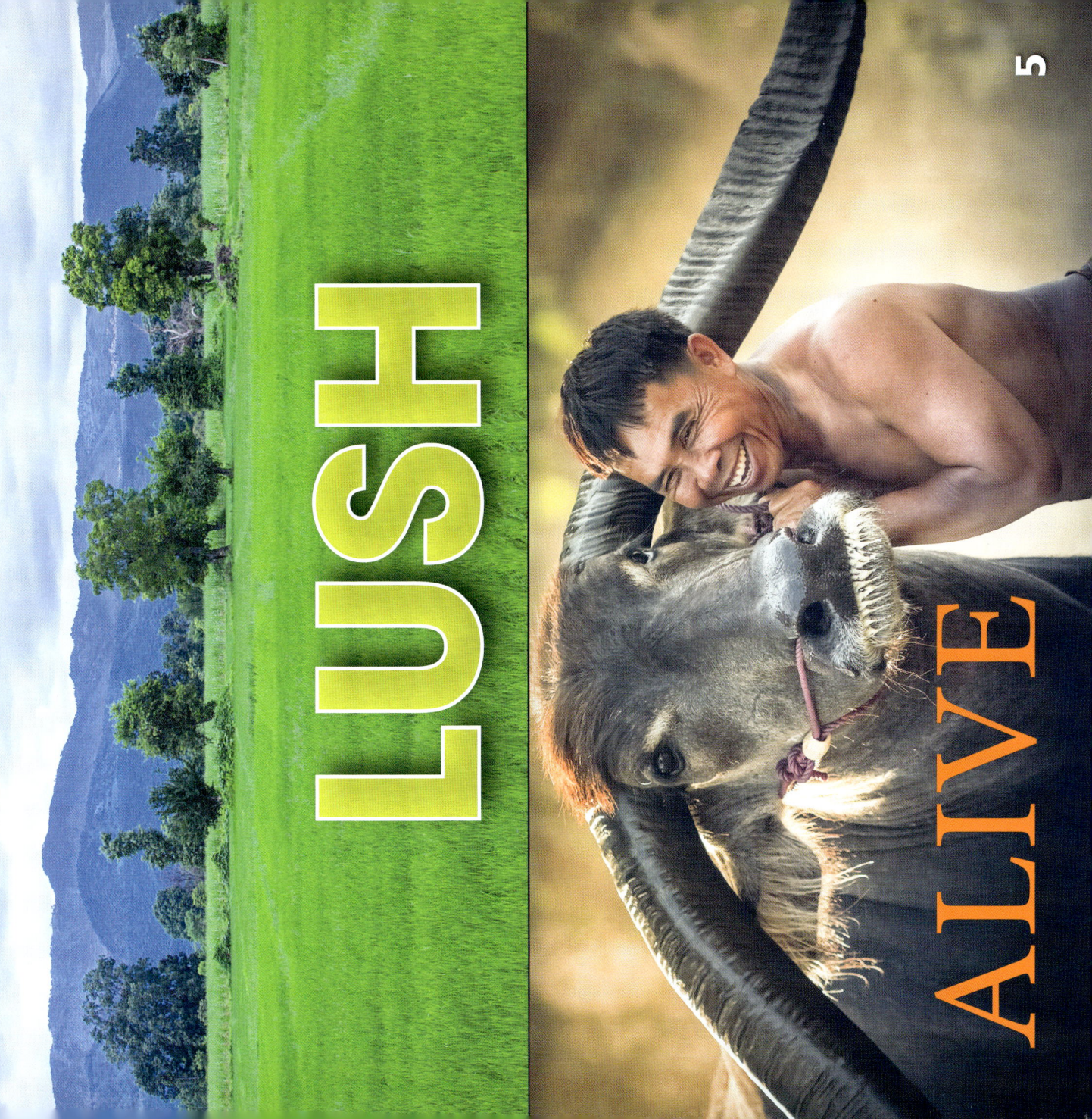

Where is Myanmar (mee-AHN-mar)?

This country is located in Southeast Asia. Over 55 million people live there.

Myanmar is also known as Burma. People from Myanmar are called Burmese.

Myanmar is warm and green. Thick jungles cover the land.

In summer, heavy rain falls. This creates good soil for farming.

Burmese farmers grow rice, beans, and sesame plants. Sesame seeds are used on hamburger buns and other foods!

close-up of sesame seeds

Beautiful animals live in Myanmar. Tigers walk along rivers.

Elephants march in forests.

Monkeys rest in treetops.

Much of Myanmar's wildlife is **endangered**. Why? People are destroying the places where the animals live.

11

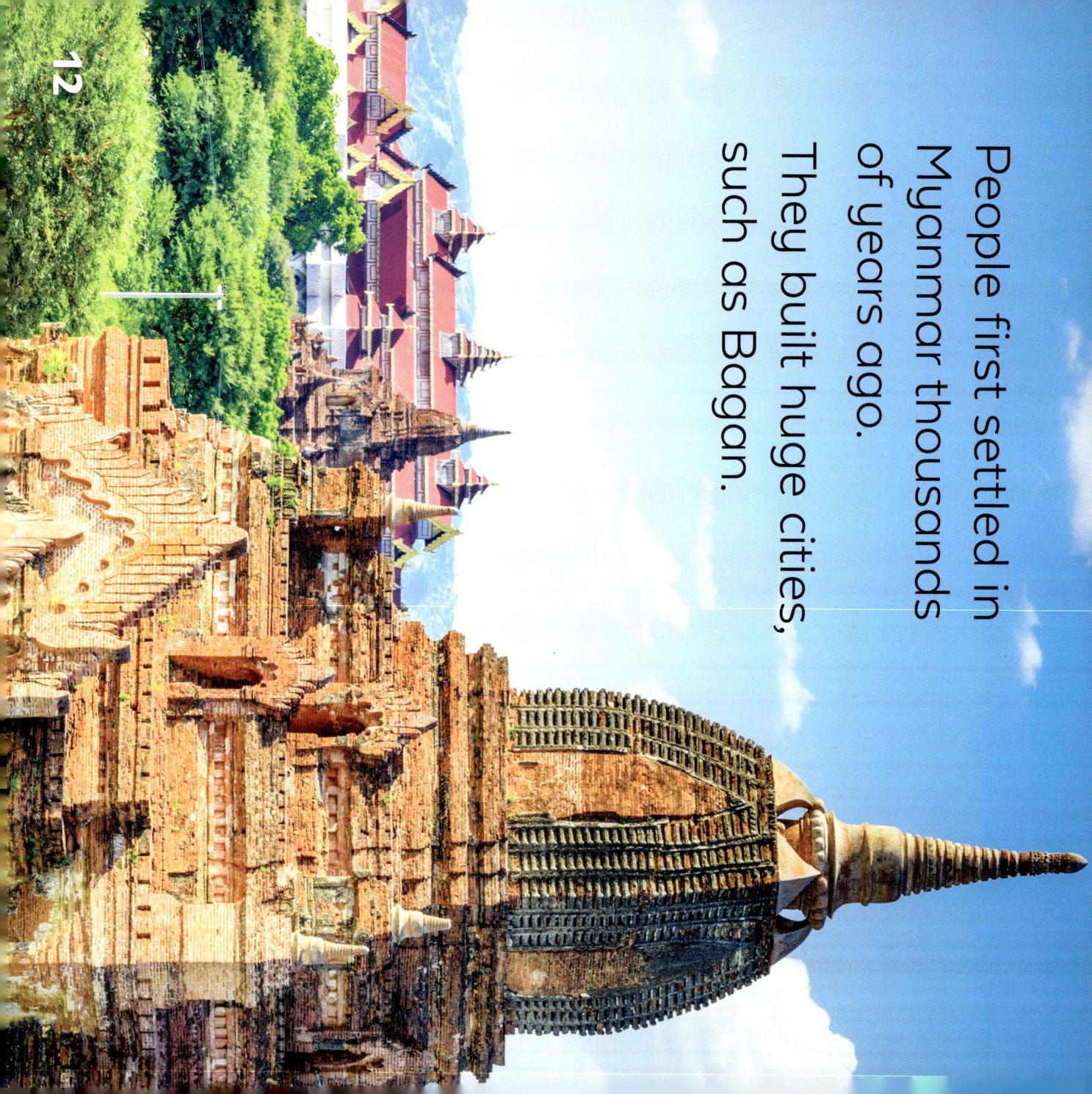

People first settled in Myanmar thousands of years ago. They built huge cities, such as Bagan.

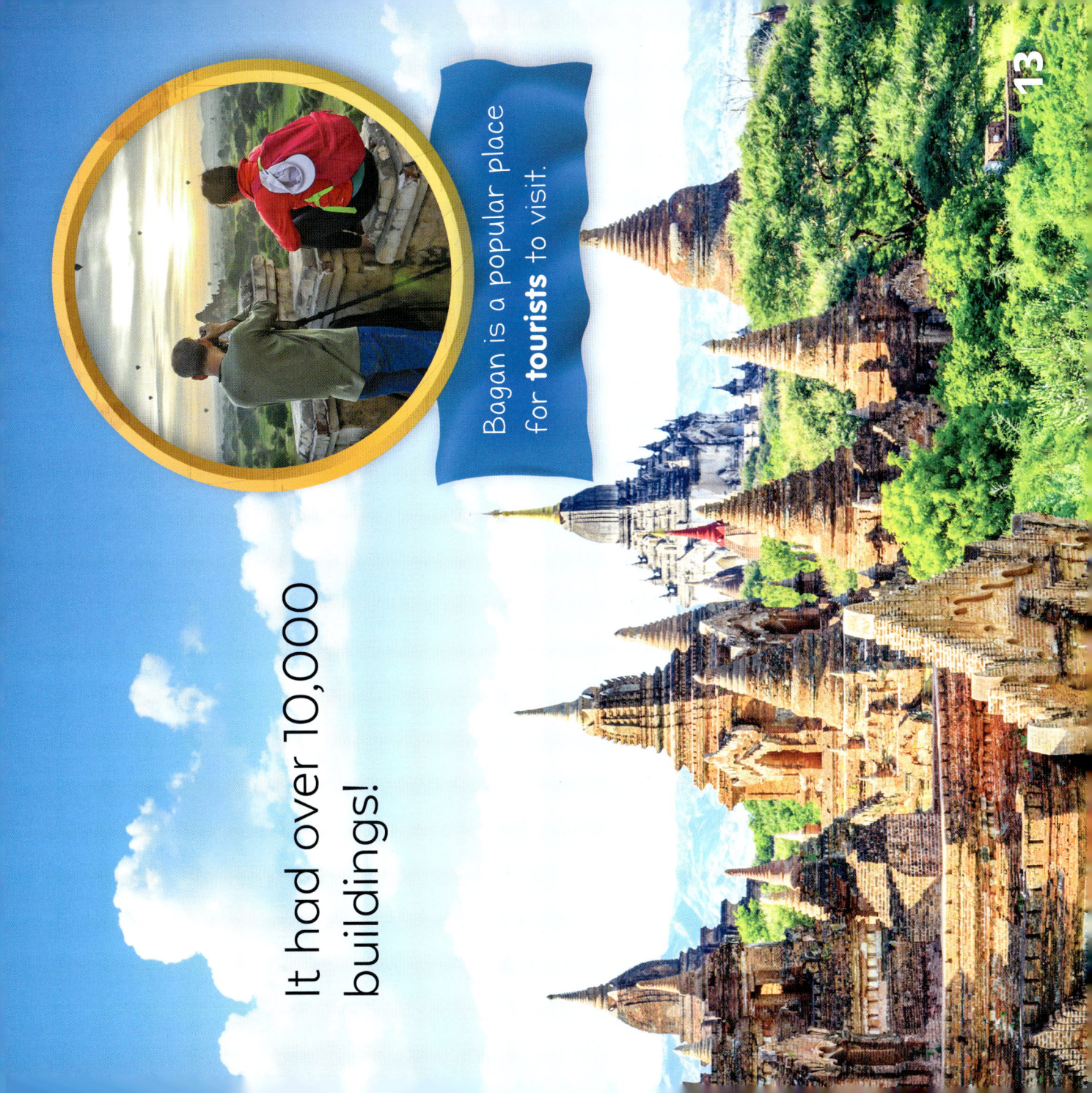

It had over 10,000 buildings!

Bagan is a popular place for **tourists** to visit.

Much later, Great Britain and Japan ruled Myanmar. The Burmese fought for their freedom.

In 1948, the country became **independent**.

However, the Burmese people are still working toward peace.

In 1989, the name of the country changed from Burma to Myanmar.

Nay Pyi Taw (NAY pee daw) is Myanmar's **capital**. Around one million people live there.

Yangon

Yangon is the country's biggest city. It's home to over five million people.

People love to visit Yangon's markets. There, they can buy food, flowers, and much more!

Religion is an important part of Burmese life. Most people practice Buddhism.

They worship in stunning **pagodas**. Some look like giant golden bells.

Shwedagon Pagoda

The Shwedagon Pagoda is covered with 4,500 diamonds!

Burmese is the main language of Myanmar.
It has its own alphabet!
This is how you say *hello* in Burmese: မင်္ဂလာပါ (MIN-ga-la-ba)

Around 100 different languages are spoken in Myanmar.

Burmese food is delicious! *Mohinga* is a rich fish soup. It's often served for breakfast.

mohinga

tea leaf salad

Tea isn't just for drinking! In Myanmar, tea leaf salad is a common snack.

What do people do for fun in Myanmar?

Burmese love soccer.

Another favorite sport is *chinlone*, or caneball.

It's like soccer but played with a woven ball.

A caneball is made from rattan, a kind of woody vine.

The sun is strong in Myanmar. How do people protect their skin from sunburn? They use *thanaka* paste.

It's made from ground tree bark!

Some people make designs on their skin with thanaka paste.

27

Myanmar's festivals make a splash!

The Thingyan water festival takes place in April. It marks the Buddhist New Year. People throw water at each other to celebrate.

The Festival of Lights is held in November. People attach candles to balloons and let them go!

Fast Facts

Capital city: Nay Pyi Taw

Population of Myanmar: Over 55 million

Main language: Burmese

Money: Kyat

Major religion: Buddhism

Neighboring countries: Bangladesh, China, India, Laos, and Thailand

Cool Fact: Many Burmese men wear long skirts called *longyis*.

Glossary

capital (KAP-uh-tuhl) the city where a country's government is based

endangered (en-DAYN-jurd) in danger of dying out

independent (in-di-PEN-duhnt) free of control from others

pagodas (puh-GOH-duhz) Buddhist buildings used for worship

tourists (TOOR-ists) people who travel and visit places for pleasure

Index

animals 9, 10–11
capital 16, 30
cities 12, 16–17
festivals 28–29
food 9, 22–23
history 12–13, 14–15
land 8–9
language 20–21, 30
population 6, 16–17, 30
religion 18–19, 30
sports 24–25

Read More

Mara, Wil. *Myanmar (Enchantment of the World).* New York: Scholastic (2016).

Yip, Dora. *Welcome to Myanmar (Welcome to My Country).* New York: Gareth Stevens (2001).

Learn More Online

To learn more about Myanmar, visit
www.bearportpublishing.com/CountriesWeComeFrom

About the Author

Anastasiya Vasilyeva lives in New York City. She loves learning about new countries and trying different cuisines. One day soon, she hopes to taste Burmese food.